Aaron Spira

As above,
      So below.
As within,
      So without.

With wit, courage, tenderness, and honesty, John Walcutt has created a book that can (and should) be read over and over. It expresses so many truths not just about acting, but about how to lead an open-hearted, unpretentious, fulfilling life. While acknowledging that being an actor can be a royal pain in the ass (rejection much?), Walcutt's book expresses a Zen-like hope and gratitude that reminds us that the journey is the destination. Read this book now! It's like taking a bath in warm chocolate pudding. If you're into that sort of thing.

--Spencer Kayden. Actress. Two time Tony Nominee.

ZEN AND THE ART OF BEING
A PROFESSIONAL ACTOR

By
John Walcutt

FOR DUCK SOON
WHO IS A WARRIOR

Fairview Publishing Los Angeles, California
United States Copyright John Walcutt 2013
Protected by International Copyright Union
All rights reserved.
#TXu 1-887-579

Cover Designs, Drawings and Artwork by Sean Hur.
ISBN#978-0-615-98229-8

INTRODUCTION

Thirty-five years ago today, I arrived in Hollywood in my 1963 Volkswagen bug, pulling a U-Haul trailer the size of a Porta-Pottie, which contained all of my worldly possessions. I came with a dream. I wanted to be a working actor. I didn't know anyone. I wasn't connected. I didn't have a job or a place to live. But I was driven. I was dedicated. And I was dead serious. I didn't care about being a star. I had no interest in that. I wanted to be nothing but a great actor. Whatever that meant. To me, it meant being a *working* actor. I would be a working actor. My dream came true.

You probably don't know me. Might not even recognize me. But I am a professional actor. I made it. I'm living the dream. I listened to Joseph Campbell and I followed my bliss. I read Robert Frost and I took the road less traveled. I've made a living doing what I love.

I hit Hollywood at twenty-one. A small town boy from farm people in Michigan. I spent some time in the San Francisco Bay area on my way to landing here on The Boulevard Of Broken Dreams. Hit the ground running hard and never stopped. I walked down Hollywood Boulevard the night I got here, in the pouring rain. Felt like I was James Dean in that famous poster. Didn't dampen my spirits one bit. I drank the rain through my pores and the soak through my shoes, stepping on the stars in the sidewalk and planning where mine might be someday.

I drove up to Yamashiro, the Japanese restaurant with the postcard view. I parked, got out of my bug, and stood for two hours in the rain looking at the beautiful lights of The City Of Angels. I began to weep. My heart racing. My destiny. Paulo Coelho called it your "personal legend." What you were meant to do. Here I was. To be the best. To be great. To be respected by my peers and make my living as a professional actor. To be… (there was no "or not to be".) To go from stage to screen and back again. Classics and the new stuff. Movies, TV, plays. Always changing. Always growing. To work with the best. To be a professional actor, man! YES!

All I heard was "nobody makes it." All I heard was "you have to know somebody". But I did it… I did it. I've lived the life. I'm still living it. I'm not done yet. A working actor.

I've worked with the best. I've shared the screen with Oscar winners, with the world's most beautiful people. With warriors and angels and demons. Where do I start? Leonardo Di Caprio, Kate Winslett, Russell Crowe, Denzel Washington, William Shatner, Holly Hunter, Gene Hackman, Sharon Stone, Joaquin Pheonix, Steve Carell, Toni Collette, Greg Kinnear, Demi Moore, Dennis Hopper, Alec

Baldwin, Kevin Bacon (one degree of separation!), Jennifer Love Hewitt, Charlie Durning, David Carradine… Lassie. Who do you like?

In television I've worked with the best of my generation, from Michael Landon to David E. Kelley to John Wells to J.J. Abrams…
Bob Newhart and Dick Martin, to Aaron Sorkin.

I've shared the stage with Tony Award winners and played Henry V, Hamlet, Macbeth, Richard III, Mercutio; the plays of Chekhov. Worked on a new play with Beth Henley. Played Billy The Kid in Juneau, Alaska. World Premiered a musical at The Old Globe in San Diego. Worked with the best stage directors in the country including Des McAnuff, Jack O'Brien, Molly Smith and Michael Greif. On and on… I don't want to bore you. Lucky me. Lucky me.

But it wasn't luck at all. It was just hard work. Nothing but sheer, hard work. I worked harder than anyone else I know. I had to fight for everything. Audition for everything. Over and over again. To try to get in. To try to open doors. That hasn't changed.

I've always tried to work with the best people I could. Took small parts if it meant I could work with the best. I wanted to learn. To be around them. I loved it. Still do. Relentless.

It's an amazing life. A marvelous career. I wouldn't trade it for anything. I've done what so many people dream of. What people try for, but just can't hang in there. I've always known I was in it for the long run. I've had my heart broken many times. Disappointments so numerous I couldn't begin to list them… nor would I want to. It's enough to say I paid my dues. Believe me.

My first move was to get into the best class that I could. A place to work. A place to meet people and to begin to find my way. To be discovered? I went to the Strasberg School. Too, too expensive, but I knew the history. It was the kind of actor I wanted to be. To be taken seriously.

I pounded the pavement. Auditions and interviews. Just like every FOB (fresh off the boat) dreamer that gets off the planes, trains and buses in Hollywood by the thousands every year.

I answered a casting ad looking for "an authentic British kid" ("MUST BE FROM ENGLAND!") in The Dramalogue (now Backstage) actor's paper. Well, I'd never been to England, but I kind of like the Beatles… I sent in my pic and resume with a cover letter saying how I'd just arrived from across the pond; even signing off with a "cheerio!" Yes… THAT lame! But I got the call, did the interview and two auditions with my best Brit accent and weaving remarkable tales of my life in

London, and landed the role that got me my SCREEN ACTORS GUILD card: a movie called GAUGUIN THE SAVAGE, in which I played the oh-so-British son of David Carradine and Lynn Redgrave. Both of these remarkable actors took me under their wing(s), and in their own ways had great impact on my young career and life. Mr. Carradine introduced me to the world and thoughts of Zen. Sometime later, Ms. Redgrave wrote a letter of recommendation for me to get into The Royal Academy Of Dramatic Art in London. A career was born. Not a star... but a career. Just what I wanted.

Now, nearly 200 SAG principal jobs later... in leading roles as well as supporting; in Oscar winners, hits, and stinkers you've never heard of; after stage roles all over the country - leading, supporting, and carrying spears... what wisdom can I impart to you?

Well, here it is:

ZEN AND THE ART OF BEING A PROFESSIONAL ACTOR.

Building and maintaining a career as a professional actor (an artist of any kind in America, I suspect), demands an unearthly amount of drive, energy, resilience, creativity, dedication, and humor. I have spent decades on call 24/7. Fueled by ambition, and riding an emotional and financial roller coaster of effort and endurance.

And then I finally LANDED. Landed... in the Zen Way. In the here and now. And peace and joy descended upon me and I lived happily ever after. Well, sort of...

What I mean is, I woke up. I woke up to THIS MOMENT. To THIS IS IT. This is my life. Every second. Every beat. Here I am and this is me. This is what I do and this is who I am. I stopped "aspiring" and I "became". I fell into sync with my self and my life.

Like all life's journeys, and all Zen stories, I was frantically chasing one thing, only to realize, finally, that I'd achieved everything. But it took the effort to LAND. To put on the brakes and stop in the here and now.

For me, true peace has come in the realization that success is a good day. A day well lived and well spent. And that is how I live my life: from day to day, moment to moment. I do my work, whatever that is this day, with the greatest joy and fullest presence possible. And it is good. It is the fullest my life can be. And the most satisfying.

Do not misunderstand: it is not all easy, or happy, or smooth. It is what it is. I chop my wood and carry my water, as the Zen folks like to say. Doing our tasks. I stop and smell the roses. I live each moment to the fullest… Whatever cliché' you care to use. But that's what I do. Be here now.

MY THANKS

I thank, especially, anyone who was ever nice to me. I thank those who encouraged me, from the bottom of my heart. I wasn't always mature enough to thank you at the time, but I sincerely thank you now. To those who discouraged me, I thank you, too. For you also fueled my quest as I drove myself even harder to prove you wrong. And it was worth it. You made me strong. I lived through the late seventies in San Francisco, the eighties on Sunset Strip, and the nineties in the San Fernando Valley! Tough, wild times. I've been broke in New York, rich in L.A., and hobbed with the nobs on champagne and caviar. But nothing beats the highs of an acting career. How can I describe to you the rush of my first standing ovation on opening night as Hamlet? Or shooting baskets with George Clooney between takes? Standing on the deck of the Titanic with Leo, Kate, and Jim? Reading a film script across the table from Gene Hackman? Or sitting in cast chairs with Dennis Hopper as the sun sets magnificently pink and orange over an Indian Reservation in New Mexico, and Mr. Hopper regales me with tales of working with the likes of James Dean, Paul Newman, Natalie Wood and Marlon Brando? Mind blowing.

For these moments I am truly thankful. For these moments it was all well worth it. For these moments have been what it is all about for me. Being a professional actor. It is these moments I'll always treasure. Even if they had never paid me to be there.

And that is what I have to give to you, my friends. That one idea: savor the moment. Every moment. The old cliché' is true: it goes fast. It's hard and it's fast. So slow it down. Enjoy it. Love it. And treasure every moment. This IS your journey. As every Zen Master will tell you: it's not the destination. Life is in the journey. Here you are. Right here. Right now.

Here you are.

ZEN AND THE ART OF BEING A PROFESSIONAL ACTOR.

MY SPECIAL THANKS

For you who have opened my eyes. Held my hand. Laughed at my jokes. Said "yes". Said "wonderful". Been there. Gave to me. Inspired me. Pushed me. Gave me a chance… I thank you.

My dad.

Al Blair. Nancy Allen. Laurie, Judith, and Lynnda.
Dakin Matthews. Lee Shallat Chemel, Joe Stern, Martin Benson, Stephen Elliott, Alice Hirson, Cindy Gilmore, Matthew Lesher, Kim Dorr-Tilley, Craig Noel, Jack O'Brien, Des McAnuff, Andrew J. Traister, John Patterson, Michael Landon, David Carradine, Lynn Redgrave, Don Hahn, Hrach Titizian, Don Johnson, Mark Neal, Dennis Hopper, Bobby Moresco, Sam Alarcon, Bill Hoffman, Catherine Fitzmaurice, Robert Hays, Steve Harris, Tom Bradac…

And Jeffrey Tambor.

And to Duck Soon, my dear wife, who made this book possible.

And a very special thank you to Sean Hur, whose cover designs, artwork, and eye have made this book beautiful.

John Walcutt   2013   Hollywood, California

Career

It is a Ferris Wheel.

　Sometimes you are up, and sometimes

You are at the very bottom.

　But if you STAY on the ride...

Well, of course, it could

　Totally break down.

August 25th, 2017

Living in Oblivion "

by Tom Dicillo
(writer and director)

1997

Short indie film about making an indie film

- Young lanister dwarf in "Dream sequence"
- Steve Buscemi plays director, his first film

Explores a variety of shot-types and
blocking changes, and dealing w/ big actors

listening

Understand the difference between

Insight

And information.

1st September 2017

Revolutionizing technology and digitization

Take - An attempt to get the shot, repeated until satisfied

Shots - The setup of the scene and the angle it is being Film from

Scenes - An idea of what is happening

Documentary about Stanley Kubrick

Stanley Kubrick
"A Life in Pictures"

Lived 1928-1999

Zeitgeist - feeling of the times

Zeitgeist = feeling of the times

SHOT COMPOSITION

Mise en scene

the greatest explores
post cold war fears →

Scandilis →

Broke
genre norms →

About 18th
NASA cent.
Used a lense
with f-stop 0.7 →

Works:
- Fear and Desire
- Killer's kiss
- Spartacus
- Dr. Strangelove
- Lolita
- 2001 Space Odysee
- A Clockwork Orange
- Barry Lyndon
- The Shining
- Full Metal Jacket
- Eyes Wide Shut

Coverage - All shots at a place
Master shot - Establishing shot ? - Like the beginning and end wide shot for a ~~scene~~
Two shot - Two people in a shot
Over the shoulder - Dirty - includes shoulder
Clean - doesn't include shoulder

warrior

*Make no mistake about it:
to be a professional actor in America
you have to be a warrior. I suit up
every day to go to war. I fight not only
for my art, but for my survival.*

8th September 2017

Allison Anders

- Hard upbringing, raped at 12 by uncle
- Grew up in trailer parks in new mexico raising kids on her own later
- Scholarship at LACC taking film classes — Jason Lee / Spike Jones
- Collabed with 2 other film guys to make "Mi Vida Loca" about girl gangs at echo park in LA, 1993 Sundance Film Festival

- Large portions of budget goes to paying actors and locations
To keep non-union actors happy, feed them well

Mi Vida Loca — authenticity

- Beautifully composed shots, artistically fantastic
  - Uses many photography theories to compose shots
- All actors and actresses are not skilled or experienced but they are just playing the role of themselves so it seems natural
  - Lots of narration
- Shit's real as fuck
- ✱ Ernesto dies and they get McDonalds
- It's enthralling while maintaining a sense of mundanity through bringing you in to the "slice of life"
- Amazing that none of the actors are payed, all non-union

Funeral Count: ///

Allison Anders — Mi Vida Loca
1993 — Sundance Film Festival
NY Critic's Circle Prizes
Bought by HBO for $5 mil, forced her to add chipper

Robert Towndsend
Hollywood Shuffle
1987
Director, Writer, Producer
MGM

optimist

- Funded his first movie on his credit cards ($100K)
- Started a production company
  • Uses it to help people from disadvantaged backgrounds

肯

Nichi Nichi Kore Ko Nichi.

-Every day is a beautiful day.

Snoop Dog's
Soul Plane

15th September, 2017

Zeitgeist - 1980's

Coverage - Very little individual coverage, mostly zoomed back group shots. Individual shots were very artistic

Loose Endo (Film Stock) - The unused pieces of film at the end of a film cartridge

---

Hollywood Shuffle

Robert Townsend   1987

- Everything filmed on Loose Endo film stock in a single take
- Bought by MGM for $5 mil after 11 months
- Light-hearted yet real, lots of pop culture references

Zeitgeist of the 1980's
- Commentary of how black people were treated in the film industry

Steven Soderbergh
Sex, Lies, and Videotape
1989
Writer, Director, Producer, DP, Editor
structure Best Film / Best Actor — Cannes

基

* James Spader — Young Redding
Andie MacDowell

Laura San Giacomo
Peter Gallagher

Academy Award Nom — Best Screenplay and Best Actor

Produced | Oceans 8, 10, 11, 12, 13
Pleasanville | Erin Brockanch
Michael Clayton | Traffic | Lucky Logan
 | Out of Sight | Kafka
 | Magic Mike
 | Contagion

You must create structure where
there is none.
    And then you must create freedom
within that structure.

Intimacy

Quiet

Satiated a starving crowd

Shots dragged towards characters starting in moments of tension

$$\lim_{x \to 0^+} \left(\frac{\sin(x)}{x} \right)^{1/x^2}$$

$$= \lim_{x \to 0^+} \frac{1}{x^2} \ln\left(\frac{\sin(x)}{x} \right) = \lim_{x \to 0^+} \frac{\ln\left(\frac{\sin(x)}{x} \right)}{x^2} = \frac{0}{0}$$

$$= \lim_{x \to 0^+} \frac{\frac{x}{\sin(x)} \cdot \frac{x\cos(x) - \sin(x)}{x^2}}{2x}$$

Robert Rodriguez

Writer, Director, DP, Editor, Producer

1992 "El Mariachi"

failure

Won Sundance
Grand Jury Prize
Audience Prize

Made for $7k Bought by
Columbia Pictures

失

Desperado
Once Upon a Time In Mexico
Dawn to Dusk
Sin City
Spy Kids
Machete
Planet Terror

Sharkboy and Vavagirl

Pan - Moving camera side to side
Zoom - Moving camera closer
Jump Cut -
Push in (close up) -
Whip (pan) - Quickly and abruptly panning
Hand Held Camera

In baseball, a great hitter is
successful three times out of ten tries.
For an actor, to be successful, one
great hit in one hundred tries is
a miracle.

Easy Rider 1969
 Dennis Hopper
Peter Fonda
Jack Nicholson
First $100 M Indie
success Boxoffice hit
Bought by
 Columbia Pictures

成

Oscar Nom - Best Screen Play
Oscar Nom - Best Supporting Actor - Nicholson
Cannes Festival First Film Awarded
New Star Award - Nicholson

Zeitgeist | In the National Film Registry,
Soundtrack | the United States National Film Preservation
| Board's selection of films for the
| Preservation in the Library of Congress

Lense Flores - Light refraction through the lense creating weird light effects
"Fast Forward" Jump Cuts - As you change scenes, it kind of Flickers/Flashes through
Exposed Film Stock - They dropped the film stock and it got exposed between screens
Improvised Dialogue - Someone dropped acid and the director got him to break down

Waking up every morning

and looking forward to your day

whatever you make of it.

A modern western -
Wyatt Earp & Billy the Kid

J.J. Abrahams - Lots of lens flares

Billy Bob Thorton

"Sling Blade" 1996
Writer, director, Producer, Star
-Oscar for Screenplay
-Oscar nomination for best actor
        Cost $300k
        Made $34m
irony
    Also stars:
        -Lucas Black (first film)
        -Dwight Yoakum - Country Singer
        -John Ritter - TV star
        -Robert Duvall - The Godfather
                    Apocalypse Now   1 day

Miramax Films -
    Harvey Weinstein
Scored big in 1989 with
"Sex, Lies, and Videotape". Now
had become the most powerful
buyer and distributed of Indie
Films. Later the Miramax
name was sold to disney, and
the Weinstein Company was formed.

反

You must cultivate a ferociously
thick skin.
        You must maintain a completely
vulnerable heart.

"Essence"
Impression Authenticity

"Crafting"
Impression Creation

If I ask what is the "strength" of a movie,
don't answer with the plot, give specific details
about the cinematography

"My Big Fat Greek Wedding" 2002

Written by and Starring

Nia Vardahlos
from her play.
Oscar nom for best screenplay

challenge

With:
Jon Corbet
Michael Constantine
Joey Fatone
Lainie Kazan
Ian Gomez

Directed by TV director Joel Zwick

跳

Produced by Tom Hanks + Rita Wilson

Strengths: Script, comedy, Relatability, good message,
good late movie film
Window into Greek Culture. MUSIC

You can't join the Union unless
you're in a Union project.
You can't be in a Union project
unless you've joined the Union.

problem

It is an art that deals in life experience,
and a business that trades in youth.

Midterm   95

#1

A - ~~Steven Soderberg 1984~~ Tom Dicillo, 1983
B - ~~Robert Townsend 1988~~ Director not listed here
C - Allison Andres, 1993
D - Steven Soderberg, 1989
E - Robert Townsend, 1987
F - Robert Rodriguez, 1992
G - Dennis Hopper, 1969
H - Billy Bob Thornton, 1996
I - Joel Zwick, 2002

#2   5

- Dr. Strangelove
- 2001: A Space Odyssee
- Full Metal Jacket
- The Shining
- Barry Lyndon

#3   10

The term "Zeitgeist" refers to a feeling of the times that is apparent in certain films, often adding contextual meaning and background into character motivations. Easy Rider is an example of a film that functions well primarily because it portrays the Zeitgeist so well, in that they do lots of drugs and try to just live off the land and abandon the "system".

#4

- The fact he put together El Mariachi for $7k is amazing
- His use of jumpcuts and whip panning adds a layer of movement and space that few directors can match
- Its refreshing to know that the director of my favorite childhood films, Spy Kids and Sharkboy and Lava Girl, also has artistic talent and can make films for adults

#5   15

Zoom - Changing a shot while filming from wide to closer
Pan - Moving a shot horizontally while filming
Dolly Shot - Moving Camera on a cart while filming
Room Tone - A sound recording for editing use
Coverage - Different shots used for scene building in editing

5

#6 →

simple

One of the crucial truths about being a great actor,
is that you mustn't seem like an actor at all.

#6

My Big Fat Greek Wedding   5

Script, comedy, relatability, good message, good date film, window into greek culture

Easy Rider   5

The "go with the flow" making of this movie where they keep all the lens flares, jump cuts, *fast forward*, exposed film stock, and taking actual drugs throughout the making made this film strange yet utterly amazing. The zeitgeist was authentic.

Sex, Lies, and Videotape   5

I feel that James Spader was the source of this movie's success, because I cannot imagine any other actor that could really embody the character as Spader did. I suppose the single greatest strength of the movie, in this regard, is authenticity between the actors/actresses and the character they play.

Where is #4?
(Asked for 4)

Where is movie #4?
(Asked for 4)

the odds

If 95% of Sag-Aftra is unemployed at any given time, and less than 5% makes $5,000 a year, perhaps you have a better chance of winning the lottery and being struck by lightening on the same day, than of making a living as a professional actor.

Steven Spielberg (Duel 1971)

Jaws 1975
Close Encounters 1977
Raiders of the Lost Arc 1981
E.T. 1982
Jurassic Park 1993
Indiana Jones

(Nearly $10B in world wide sales)

Schindler's List *
The Color Purple
Saving Private Ryan

Amistaad, Bridge of Spies,
Lincoln...

*Oscars

Duel - 1971

- T.V. Movie of the Week
- Zeitgeist "Everything is going to shit and none of it is my fault"

determination

The more everyone told me that almost no one makes it as a professional actor, the more I thought the "almost" applied to me.

2005

Nicky's Birthday Camera

by John Walcutt

Zeitgeist: Huge Evolution in video/digital technology
camera "chips" (video) to digital. Pro-sumer Professional consumer Cameras -
Final Cut Editing Software - First cheap editing software
Massive surge in Reality TV.
New Sag-Aftra Contracts

Editor first gave him a beautiful cut, but he sent it back and said "I want it to look like a very sharp 12 year old boy just got "Final Cut" and made a fun project"

illusion

Bowling for Columbine
Michael Moore 2002

Acting is the only business I know
where you can die of encouragement.

"Sicko" Health Care System (2007)

"Where to Invade Next" (2015)

"Trumpland" (2016) predicted Trump's Win

"Farenheit 11/9" (coming 2018)
About what the election says
about current U.S. politics

"On Broadway" Live NY Stage Show

Michael Moore

Born in Flint, Michigan
A journalist
Makes Films for change

"Roger and Me" About General Motors (1989)
#1 commercial Doc. ever. Won every prize.

"Bowling for Columbine" Guns + Media (2002)
#1 commercial doc of all time. Oscar

"Farenheit 9/11" About 9/11 and G.W. Bush
#1 commercial doc of all time (still) Oscar Nom

subjective

 I have received feedback that I was "too handsome" and "not handsome enough" for a role,
 from two people who were in the same room at the same audition...
 more than once.

Disaster Artist

AFI
USC } Top 10 movie lists

Buster Keaton - The General
1926

Lifetime Oscar award after being found by lucile ball

motivation

If you want to get rich, invent
software.
If you want to get famous, shoot
a politician...
preferably a bad one.

(I'm kidding, of course. Don't shoot anyone.
There are too many guns. Just get rid of them.)

Final →

focus

集

*For something to fall back on,
I built up the muscles in my ass.*

1) What was the most impressive acheivement in the General?

I think it was really impressive for Buster Keaton to be able to display so much emotion, and such a full storyline with no audible dialog, and still make it rich enough and so full of life that it still resonates with young audiences today, which I have not seen from any other 90 year old movies.

2) 3 Things that made the General the most expensive movie ever made.

They had to have 3 trains in the movie at once and one of those trains got destroyed. The whole movie was basically people destroying things, and things cost money. Lastly, there must have been thousands of extras in the last battle scene, and hundreds throughout the duration of the Film as North/South battalions.

3) 3 most interesting/important things learned about Films/Film making.

- Quality Films can be made with little money by substituting costs with creative innovation.
- Some of the best movies are boring until the very end.
- The use of zeitgeist can allow for some otherwise outlandish creative choices.

support

支

The most important thing an
actor can have going for them?
Wealthy parents.

honesty

真

"*Acting is 99% honesty.*
And if you can fake that,
you've got it made."
-George Burns

efficiency

能

Good acting is fast.

Great acting is faster.

- *TV Director Aphorism*

zen

修

If you train relentlessly with the best
instructors in the field, and dedicate
yourself to the rigors of a brutal
work ethic while always keeping a
positive attitude; and if you invest
in your education and business like a
young doctor and you have the
devotion and focus of a Tibetan
monk... for decades...
You will, at least, have done that.

perspective

觀

"...Well, it's gotta be better than farmin'..."

-my father's response to my announcing that I wanted to be an actor.

fairness

If your audition is clearly the best...

You will occasionally get the part.

random

散

It isn't fair.
And it isn't progressive.

cliché

陳

Less is more.

They love to say this. But it isn't always true. More often, the meaning is: less is more…inside. MORE inside. Not less. But inside.

connections

結

It's not who you know...

but that certainly doesn't hurt.

humility

Every day of my life

is a lesson in humility.

longevity

长

Audition for a career,

not for a role.

persistence

The one common quality I see in actors who have really built a career is persistence. They just- for better or worse- never, ever gave up.

openness

Committing yourself to a life as an actor, is committing yourself to a life as a student.

gardening

Don't worry about the flowers.

Just keep watering the roots.

Or plant new seeds.

doing

行

Dancers dance. Writers write.
Singers sing. Musicians play.
The challenge for actors is:
"What do I do today?"

presence

The best acting is always present. In the here and now. The one constant among all the great actors I've worked with, is that they each made <u>me</u> feel like a great actor. They hung on my every word, my every nuance. They were very present.

change

On stage you give a performance.

On camera you have an experience.

confidence

It's confidence.

That's what it is. The one thing you

Cannot succeed without.

talent

能

Can you teach someone to be a great actor? No. It's a gift. You can teach skills. You can help and guide someone with drive and talent and confidence to be a good actor.

will

意

All through my twenties and thirties, I wrote in a journal every day what I did that day "to become a great actor."

The old cliché about an acting career:

"Who's John Walcutt?

Get me John Walcutt!

Get me a young John Walcutt!

Who's John Walcutt?"

only applies if you were very, very

successful.

effort

努

The only thing that is not subjective

is my effort.

skill

能

The only thing I'm really good at is

understanding people.

purpose

的

What do you have to <u>say?</u>

As an artist.

As a person.

As a woman.

As a man.

self

"They went with a name."

"They went with a person of color."

Alas, I have no name.

Alas, I have no color.

They want to take my name.

They want to neutralize my color.

theatre

劇場

I'm sorry, but theatre is elitist in this country. No one I know can afford the price of a ticket. Half of my life I couldn't afford the price of a ticket.

So, they have to do plays for old people.

statistics

If I had a dollar for every role I tried for and didn't get over the past thirty-five years, I think I'd just about have made the same money as I made with the roles I did get...

And I consider that a measure of my great success.

弄

When people have asked me over the years : "What have I seen you in?" or "Where have I seen you before?" or "I know you from somewhere..." "You look familiar..."

I always respond with a sly smile: "Do you watch a lot of pornography?"

Priceless.

control

制

If I do something good today,

it will have been a good day.

learning

Everyone I meet teaches me something...

Although not always what they think they are teaching me.

values

値

When I was a young actor, all I secretly said to myself was "I want to be a great actor!"

Now, what I hear from young actors is "I want to be famous."

the way

There is no road ahead of you. It is uncharted. But if you put down a brick a day, every day, one day you will look up, look back, and you will have built a road behind you.

reason

据

Why?

Why would you want to do this?

faith

Karma... I want to believe in Karma.
God... I want to believe there is God.

But all I really <u>know</u> is that if I do something good today, then something good occurred.

I am the miracle. I am the event.

strategy

Rearranging deck chairs on the

TITANIC.

worry

忱

Banging my head against the fourth wall.

wanting

There is no aspiring.

You should <u>be</u> who you are. You should

<u>be</u> the actor you want to be.

respect

I never dreamt of being a star.

My dream was to be a working actor.

My dream came true.

money

钱

They don't pay me to act.

I act because it's what I love to do.

They pay me for all they put me

through to get the job.

wisdom

智

*Actors are smart. The good ones.
I don't know any dumb actors. They are
smart and curious. And sometimes
they've been broken, or come from
broken places. They have mileage.
Mileage is very attractive. It's an
advantage... to have those dark places
to go back to. Depth, damage,
darkness... all money in the bank in our
business.*

youth

少

When I was younger, sometimes my subtext was so loud I couldn't hear my cue.

false idols

偽像

If a Director says to me:

"You're character would never do that",

My response is usually:

"My Director would never say that."

comedy

喜

People who are funny get to do comedy.

life

生

If I need to laugh in a role,

I think of my life.

If I need to cry in a role,

I think of my life.

profit

利

Honestly, the only time I feel like a loser is when I have to sit down with my taxman and list my deductions.

luck

福

I have never had an ounce of luck.
I've just worked harder than anyone
else I know.

sacrifice

犠義

If I told you that the price of your dreams might be compromise, sacrifice, obsession--you're nodding with enthusiasm—loss of friends. Bankruptcy, living like a grad student in your forties, failed marriages, ulcers, and addictions... would you still want to do this?

reveal

現

Acting is:

"This is what it's like to be <u>ME!</u>"

When I was a young actor, there was a popular text book, required reading in theatre programs, called ACTING IS BELIEVING".

Spencer Tracy said: "Acting is listening."

Antonin Artaud wrote: "Acting is setting yourself on fire and signaling through the flames what it's like."

Brando said: "Acting is not an occupation suitable for a grown man."

Jack Lemmon exclaimed through tears in front of an audience: " This is a noble profession!"

Bruce Dern told me: "It's the ability to be publicly private."

If an actor falls in the forest, is there applause?

motivation

I was invisible in my first acting classes. Shy, polite, Midwestern, modest. All the attention was on the "hot" guys, and the "hot" girls; those who were siblings or vaguely connected to famous or powerful people.

No one paid any attention to me at all. I wrote in my journal "someday these people will be telling their kids they knew me." And I put all of it into my work: the hurt, the slight, the love, the lust, the rage, the drive, the hope, the creativity... all of it... I poured into my work. I didn't <u>say</u> anything about it. I just did it.

Where are they all now? The big fish in those little ponds... I can't remember any of their names now.

It really is most like boxing. Yes, you practice madly. You train hard and relentlessly. You condition and practice your technique, your skills... over and over and over.

But when you get in the ring, you'd better be present and in the moment; connected to your opponent. Your preparation gets you to the first moment. Then, it's improvisation. You'd better be present or you'll get knocked on your ass.

Old actors used to talk about paying your dues. "Making the rounds". "Pounding the pavement..." Going to casting directors' and agents' offices and introducing yourself and personally delivering pictures and resumes, often cookies and flowers. Doors slamming in your face. Being relentless. But you had to do it. It was the best way. It's a people business.

Now, all that's impossible. But you know what? You <u>still</u> have to do it. And it's <u>still</u> a people business.

Los Angeles is the Big Leagues. The Olympic Games. It's the biggest pool of talent in the world. Everyone who becomes a star in any country in the world, comes here. It's the next rung on the ladder. Hollywood. All roads lead here. The best of the best, and the mess of the rest. So what would make you possibly think that you don't have to train and compete on the same level as an Olympic Athlete? Or have less commitment? You do! You actually need MORE. The struggle is even more fierce for actors, because everyone thinks they can act.

Unfortunately, there are no pre-qualifying times or distances, and no elimination heats in our business. It's purely attrition. How long can you hang in there before you just drop like an under-conditioned, dehydrated marathon wanna be?

seasons

It comes and it goes. It comes and it goes. Enjoy it when it's here, and prepare for when it's not.

evolution

"It takes 20 years in Los Angeles to become an actor."

-Jack Nicholson

solitude

My journey has been profoundly
singular. Perhaps to my detriment. I
have always been surrounded by
friends, and acquaintances, but it's very
clear to me that I have always been –
without question- alone in this.

care

眷

To survive in this business, you have to have good hobbies. You have to build yourself a life, an oasis, and a strong work ethic. A sound philosophy is helpful. Some faith... in something.

Because if you start to attach your self-worth to getting jobs, you're dead.

cycles

循

The curse of the unemployed actor:

"I'm an optimist in the morning

and a pessimist at night."

unemployment

失職

A few years ago, I'd just closed a summer season of Shakespeare. I was back in Los Angeles and required to go to the Unemployment Office to re-open my claim for benefits. Yes, this was in the days when they would actually talk to you. And they made me sit through a slide presentation with other non-actor unemployed applicants. The title of the presentation was "Are you searching for today's jobs with yesterday's skills?"

Yes, I thought... Iambic pentameter.

art

I can't control the business.
I can't control the casting.
I can't control the criticism
Or my income.

I can only control my work. It
really is everything to me. All I have.
The be all and the end all.

My solution has always been to
just keep doing the work.

There can be this voice in your head in the morning. This mournful insidious voice that says "Nothing good can happen to me today." It is the voice of fear. The fear of going nowhere. The despair of not having anything happening.

The only way to fight that fear, to mute that voice, is to <u>do</u> something positive. Send out pictures and resumes. Take cookies to your agent. Write a letter. Work on a scene. Read a play. See a movie. Go to the gym. Play the guitar. Take a yoga class. Dance. And for god's sake, DAYDREAM! Daydream until you bleed!

tools

A job with some flexibility.

A place that is peaceful.

Friends who are supportive and going in the right direction...

These, too, are tools of the trade.

love

If I told you that you would never

make any money, would you still do it?

It really is like the profession of baseball. Your chances of making it to the pros. The rate of failure. The grind of Zen Mind, Beginner's Mind.

The joy of being "up for a cup of coffee"*, never mind the chances of having a long career, health insurance, or a pension.

The relentless day in and day out of the long season. Playing through loss, injury, depression. Staying healthy. Staying ready and in shape. Constant training and tuning. Staying "within yourself" when the inevitable slumps hit. Celebrating the wins. Blowing off the losses. Every day is a new day. Forget about that last strikeout, this is a new at bat, a new chance to get a hit.

Being present in each moment and not haunted by what's come before. Calm and focused. Performing.

Bouncing back. Winning and losing. Everyone losses. Everyone strikes out...a lot. Even the very best. It's how you bounce back.

There are the stars. The gifted. The lucky. And the ones who work harder than anyone. The super humans. There are the utility players. Part of the team and <u>in the major leagues!</u> In the pros and playing with the best.

There is the eventual graying. It is a young person's game. Time marches on. The baton is passed...

And in the end, it is the privilege of having played the game at all. You were lucky. You were blessed. You played in the "Bigs."

*A baseball term for getting a very brief shot in The Major Leagues, up from the Minors for "a cup of coffee".

It's easy to see your life as an endless daily struggle to "get jobs". Overwhelming rejection. Constant failure, punctuated by fissures of success (hopefully), and the ever-dripping honey of encouragement. It took me a dozen years to quiet the "That's it! I'll never get another job!" voice in my head. It took me fifteen years to even realize that I had a career. The struggle, the missteps and shadows never go away completely. The doubts. Even now, if I'm not careful, when my eighty year old father begins every phone call with his inevitable "Are you gainfully employed?" jest, it can send me down the rabbit hole.

I've read them all. Every acting book. Every book about the business.

The best book about acting? ZEN MIND, BEGINNER'S MIND, by Shunryu Suzuki. Substitute the word "acting" for his word "zazen" and there you have it. I read it twice a year.

The best book about the business? OUTLIERS, by Malcolm Gladwell. Plain and simple. Put in your ten thousand hours and be at the right place at the right time.

You want to know what your career will be like? If you succeed? Read Cheryl Strayed's WILD. Then, bandage your wounds, have a cool drink of water, strap your boots back on, throw on your pack, and get right back on the trail.

Most bail right after graduation. The cliff is just too high and the abyss is just too deep. "Real" jobs and families and student loans rear their ugly heads. There is no shame in any of it.

A great thinning of the herd at 25. That quarter-century milestone and a couple of years of the reality of the hustle take down the stragglers.

At 30, all but the very toughest of the women throw in their cards and fold. Biological clock ticks like SIXTY MINUTES going to commercial, and the undeniable cruelty of our business toward the aging fem presents a Great Wall Of China at the big three oh. Often heart wrenching.

The last male exodus is at 40. Warriors. Aging boy-men worn down by decades of battle and the endless pursuit of the oh-so-near carrot. "I'm <u>this</u> close!" How many times has he said that? Tired of juggling dead-end jobs, looking for work, competitive relationships, and being on call 24/7. Or maybe it's one last presented opportunity to do something else. And they close the book and move on. Turn the page. No hard feelings. "Gave it my best shot." Better to walk away than to end up a bitter old actor. Everyone hates those. You can smell them a mile away. You can't walk from Starbucks to The Coffee Bean without tripping over a half dozen of them. All plugged in now. Writing their screenplays. Complaining about how the business "sucks" and "it ain't like it used to be." Writing that action-adventure-big-budget-drug-deal-gone-bad thriller.

And the survivors. Those who remain. Doing what they need to do to stay in the game. The lifers. Maybe lucky, relentlessly pig-headed, or just plain crazy. Maybe scored big for a minute along the way and used their money wisely. Kept their nut small. Held on to that "day job". A spouse with a real career. A house in the Valley, or a nice little apartment on the Westside... they go on. Doing what they love. Living the dream. They continue to chop wood and carry water. Day to day. "This is who I am," they say. "This is what I do." These are the winners.

Zen and the art of being a professional actor.

The joy is in the activity of the day. The quiet pride and satisfaction of being a survivor. Of knowing in your heart that you are one of the very, very few. That you are doing what you love. Work is not work. Work is joy and the reason you are. As long as you can stay in the game, there is a chance that you might score again. But that's not really what it's about.

It's the knowing that you are a veteran. That you took on all the competition, against all odds and injustice, and you did it. You competed in The Olympic Games. You played in the Big Leagues. Younger people want to be like you. The serious ones. They dream of doing what you do. Even if they've-likely- never heard of you.

There is a great inner peace in this. It is what all philosophies talk of. At any point in your journey: being in step with your life. Recognizing those moments in your life when you can say "this is who I am", "this is what I do", and "this is right where I should be."

From this comes the greatest happiness. And it doesn't matter whether it's a TV Series, an independent short, or RICHARD THE THIRD in Greenville... It's that you are doing what you were meant to do.

The price, of course, can be steep. But isn't it for all true, good things? The road might be long. But isn't it always to the most remarkable places?

And the reward? The reward is, of course, (as in all good Zen tales) the journey itself.

This vast canvas of our lives that we are painting. It's difficult to stop and get a perspective on it in progress. But when it's over, when <u>we</u> are over, all we may have is this painting we've made of this life we've lived. This journey we've traveled. Our masterpiece. And it will be titled: "THIS WAS ME".

truth

The truth is, it never was

like it used to be.

completion

完

YOU'RE ONLY FINISHED…

WHEN YOU'RE FINISHED.

LAST LOOKS

You are promised nothing.
There is no progress.
You have only the doing.

The practice itself is the reward. The struggle is the joy. Is that enough for you? Each day you chop wood and carry water. Just like The Buddha. Just like Thoreau… all of them. All of the searchers and seekers and thinkers and dreamers. But your wood is your art and your water is your business. Your daily labor and love and attention to these chores and the details <u>are</u> your life. Your life is each moment. And this one and the next one, too. Now. Here it is. It is here. Your life. And this is what you do. This is who

you are. You do not aspire to do it. Or to be it. You just do it and you are. Now. If a part of your business is being a waitress, or bartender, or car salesman, or paralegal so that you can pay your rent and have the flexibility to go to auditions, there is no shame in that. You are doing that because you are an actor. That is who you are. That is what you do. If you have no paying acting job, and make money doing something else, that is your chopping wood. That is your carrying water. It is what you do to be who you are. You are an actor. Find your place to act however you can: in class, in plays, homeless shelters, on the street corner! Here is your joy. Enjoy it and celebrate it!

As in all Zen teachings, the key is to find the joy in chopping the wood. Find the peace in carrying the water.

This is your canvas.
What will you paint today?
This is your journey.

me

Everything that I have done, I am.
Everything that I have ever done…
every win, every loss, every hurt, every
laugh, every tear, every effort, every
step has made me into the actor, the
artist, the person that I am. These are
my brushstrokes.

Without my journey, I would not be
here. Without your journey, you will
not be there.

You are promised nothing.
There is no progress.
You only have the doing.

smile

And don't forget your sense of humor...

I flew my mother, who was illiterate, to see my opening night as HAMLET. It was a big event for me, and afterward, after the three-hour performance and the standing ovation, she sat silently in my dressing room as dozens of well-wishers and congratulators swept in and out with flowers and gushes and love. Finally, when it had quieted down, we walked together to the parking lot. Still she said nothing. Just small talk, but nothing about my performance. In the car at last, after turning the key, I turned to her and could not stop myself from saying: "Mom, did you like the show?"

"Honey", she sighed in her Oklahoma drawl and turning up one side of her mouth in a twist of regret, " You know I love you. But don't make me sit through anymore of these King Arthur plays."

Every day is a lesson in humility.

A poem

And when it is over
I will be done.
And when I am done
I will be gone.

And when I am gone.
What will I have done?

Only what I did, kid.
Only what I did.

Breathe in. Breathe out.
Chop wood. Carry water.
Enjoy.

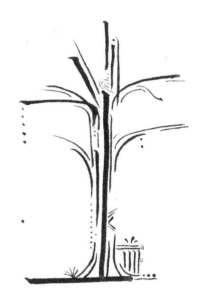

Zen and The Art of Being A Professional Actor
John Walcutt   *FAIRVIEW PUBLISHING*

Trips

2001 Space Odysee

JOHN WALCUTT is currently the Producing Artistic Director of Shakespeare Orange County, and the Founding Director of The Acting Conservatory at OCSA-The Orange County School of The Arts- both in Southern California.

He has built a wonderful career as an onscreen actor, a stage actor, a director, writer and producer, based in Los Angeles. His many fond theatre memories include dozens of shows at South Coast Repertory, The Odyssey Theatre, The Old Globe in San Diego, The La Jolla Playhouse, and The Mark Taper Forum; and various Regional Theatres across America. His favorite roles have ranged from classics such as the title roles in HAMLET, HENRY V, RICHARD II, RICHARD III, MACBETH and other Shakespeare turns as both Prince Hals, Mercutio,Cassius and Andrew Aguecheek; to leads in all the major Chekov plays, Shaw, Beckett, and Feydeau. His contemporary stage work has included the premieres of THE DIVINERS, Stephen Metcalf's musical WHITE LINEN, Beth Henley's ABUNDANCE, and the title role in THE COLLECTED WORKS OF BILLY THE KID. His favorite directors have included Craig Noel, Jack O'Brien, Michael Greif, Des Mc Anuff, Michael Kahn, Andrew Traister, Dakin Matthews, and Molly Smith. In L.A. , he is a founding member of the critically-acclaimed Antaeus Theatre Company (classical) and The Matrix Theatre Company (contemporary); and he has Guest-Starred in nearly 200 TV shows and films, including TITANIC, LITTLE MISS SUNSHINE, SEABISCUIT, LOST, GREY'S ANATOMY, THE NEWSROOM, IT'S ALWAYS SUNNY, CRIMINAL MINDS, MAD MEN, and many, many more.

His favorite TV roles have included cult-popular recurring turns as Dennis Hopper's whacked-out doctor on CRASH, Jennifer Love Hewitt's evil nemesis "Wide Brim" on GHOST WHISPERER, the struggling alcoholic father "Tom Johnson" on JAG, and the time-traveling father of Quinn (Jerry O'Connell) on SLIDERS.

John received The Golden Ace Award at The Las Vegas Film Festival for Comedy Feature Director (THE ALPHA GEEK); wrote the screenplay for the film MAKING CONTACT (BRI/BET TV), produced SEX AND A GIRL starring Robert Hays, Alison Lohman, Ellen Green, and Danny Masterson for Lifetime Television; and just received an INDIE FEST AWARD for BEST DIRECTOR for the new, scary feature TERMITE: THE WALLS HAVE EYES, which played at The Berlin, Cannes and Toronto Film Festivals, and is headed for TV in 2013.

John is very proud to have received a SCREEN ACTORS GUILD AWARD for OUTSTANDING ENSEMBLE ACTING in the film LITTLE MISS SUNSHINE, as well as Best Actor Prizes at The Houston, Sitges and 2012's Sunset International Film Festivals for 3 different film performances. His many voice over credits for Disney Feature Animation include his favorites, MULAN, DINOSAUR, and THE HUNCHBACK OF NOTRE DAME.

He has taught a sold-out professional acting class in Los Angeles for 15 years, and is currently on the faculty of Miracosta College in Oceanside, California.

Made in the USA
San Bernardino, CA
13 July 2017